BROKEN HEARTS

POETRY COLLECTION

RAJMOHAN P R

Made with ♥ on the Notion Press Platform
www.notionpress.com

Dedicate all poetry lovers.

Contents

Foreword

Dedicate all poetry lovers.

Preface

Dedicate all poetry lovers.

Acknowledgements

Dedicate all poetry lovers.

Prologue

Rajmohan.P.R

Author:-Rajmohan

Qualification:-

M.COM(Finance),DTTM,PGDCA,FDM(Google)

Kuttanellore, Thrissur,Kerala,India

Current Job: Finance officer in Middle East Based Co.

Published 11 books in English and Malayalam

e-mail:prrmohan0@gmail.com

Wife Dhanya Menon

Son Thejus R Menon

1. Never Quit from Life

Enter Caption

Ever wonder why life is so ruthless,
Making you feel that you are worthless,
All ventures ending up in tragedy and pain,
Resulting in huge losses without any gain,

Your loved ones fleeing from you unable to bear,
Your sad stories of which they don't care,
Scars inflicted all over your body by bitter words,
Piercing your heart with a thousand words,

None around you lend a helping hand,
By expect you to rise up swiping all the sand,
When all around you is fading and dark,
With none to give you an encouraging spark,

Remember...

Life tries hard to pull you down and make you lose,

Get up and move on searching for your muse,
Write your legacy each and every day,
SO that your history forever will stay,

Work until you see success within the reach,
Then will others about your path will preach,
In all that you do just be yourself,
The only thing to quit is Quitting itself.

2. My Thought

What is the time now?

It is 11:50 PM.

It's the end of the day, my eyes are heavy....

But I can't fall asleep. Thoughts are coming like rain.

As I am in bed, I try to remember

All the previous moments that occurred in my life.

I speak to myself. Then I realized...

It is not the end, I have to go on....more and more...

Life has so much to offer. But only the beginning.

God created me intentionally to do more...

God created me completely to do more...and more

Only God can justify my feeling..

3. Travel

If you want to travel around the world...

You need too much money ...

If you travel around the world.

You will get more knowledge.

You work for knowledge more than wealth.

You can't succeed until you fail.

You love life and accept failure if any.

You can't succeed until you fail.

Spend more money and time on traveling.

4. Fantasy

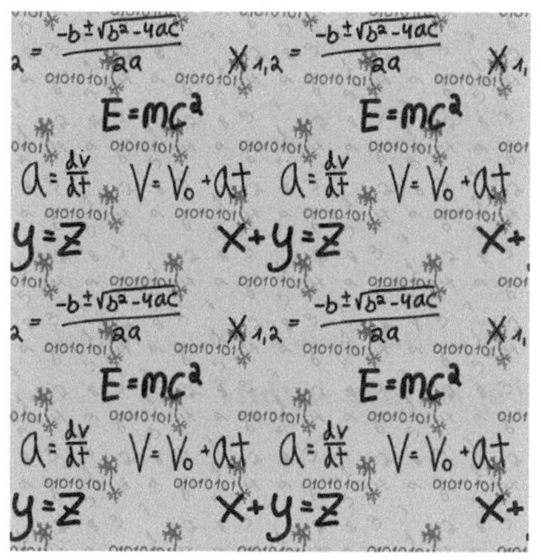

All the knowledge is yours,
Fantasy is your darshan,

Do not match with the soul,
What kind of mirror is that?

Your Generation is sad,

There is a thought of slaves.

The poison of mind should not come out,
What kind of mantra is this?

The essence of the teeth is forgotten,

Education has forgotten the promises,

Strange truth to the truth
The form of artwork.

From the confusion of the routine

Pick up the eyes and look outside.
To whom I thought to be dust,
That Sea is the one.

You have the blood of the warriors,

You are the son of blood seeds.
You have the qualities of a child...

Chapter5

Like a flower ready to cut.

Like a wind coming towards...to me...

Like a fire ... inside of you.

I will surely live with you.

Looking into your eyes....

I see myself sailing with you...

I will surely live with you....up to end...

You are in my dreams .... you can make it happen.

When you captured my hand, I felt the love in you.

I will surely live with you...

6. In Search of Love

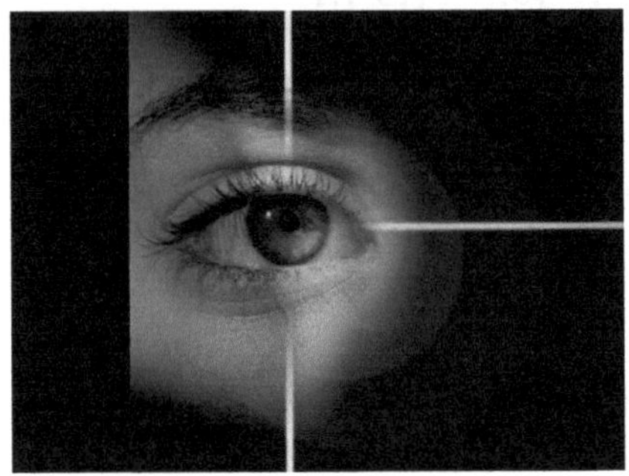

All are in search of finding true love...

Finding true love is unexpected ....

It may find out anytime....

maybe it's from the wrong place,

maybe it's the wrong time

but really it's the right person

If it's love....It's nothing right and wrong....

but love is not blind at all...

it's an unconditional finding...

The heart will say one day....

you're the one for me....

There ends the searching for LOVE...

7. My passion

My first passion is my paint brush

In my first painting, I made a flower, (of joy)

Used various colours

Did not even know the colour combination

I was a self-learner

Use to dream of nice paintings made by me

From an early age, I use to work on the sustainability of materials around me

I Used to see forms in bottles and made a doll out of it

Colours are my first love

My passion is to paint all sorts of materials in all mediums.

I worked with all mediums from charcoal to watercolour with a brush

I was madly in love with my paint brush.

Don't want to part with my first crush

8. Ancient sun

Early in the ancient space

There was an antic love

Down under the sun

We played and spy together

We played games of young love

We were together two

Early was those years

Filled with passions and dreams

Brown eyes looking in blue

We played and spy together

We played games of young love

We were together two

Eyes brown bright

In the ancient sunlight

Under the sun

Without a goodbye and anyone

9. SHADOWS

In the dark night hour, I see a pair of shadows

Declined upon a blind - a white and narrow

Their moving to and fro, their paining, their thirsting

The shadow women and the shadow man

They painfully incline their heads-but vainly

They seek to hear each other, but they can't

They may be whispering, they may be calling,

But they hear nothing, though they may be hawling

Two shadows of the night, so brief their span

Capable of touching, of conversing

Fast moving to and fro and paining,thirsting

The shadow women and the shadow man

10. The artificial World

Time runs
inside the melting pot
interrupted minds...
smell away
time is thinking
in human being
see eyes
In the artificial World

Reality minds
become artificial minds
to artificial reality
are the witness
of illusions
In the artificial World

Unhappy
little girl and boy
time runs
invisible hands
take them
into the
Artificial World...

11. Broken Hearts

The Brain Says...
No! don't approach her.
The Heart Says
Go! and get her...
Brain Says...

You Can't Love Her.
Heart Says
Put nothing above Her.
Brain Says
Look She's Breaking You.
Heart Says
Calm Down- She's Just In A Bad Mood.

Brain Says
She's Going To Leave You Behind.
Heart Says
No, you are the Only Thing On Her Mind.

Mind says....

If I could have just one wish,
I would wish to wake up every day
to the sound of your breath on my neck,
the touch of your fingers on my skin,
the warmth of your lips on my cheek,
and the feel of your heart beating with mine...
Knowing that I could never find that feeling
with anyone other than you.....

Printed by Libri Plureos GmbH in Hamburg,
Germany